What's Next After Dental School

The 8 Must Haves Every New Dentist Should Know Before They Make a Costly Mistake

Robert A. Lalor DDS

What's Next After Dental School

Printed by:
90-Minute Books
302 Martinique Drive
Winter Haven, FL 33884
www.90minutebooks.com

Copyright © 2016, Robert A. Lalor DDS

Illustrated by Alicia Roe

Published in the United States of America

150916-00240

ISBN-13: 978-0692606629
ISBN-10: 0692606629

For more information on 90-Minute Books including finding out how you can
publish your own lead generating book, visit www.90minutebooks.com or call
(863) 318-0464

Here's What's Inside...

Introduction

During the process of interviewing a number of newly graduated dentists for a position in our practice, we met a very bright woman with whom we had several engagements. As our discussions progressed, it appeared that the position was a good fit for both of us. We continued in our encounters with her and reached the point of going over a contract, and were happy to find there were very few sticking points. It appeared that it would be a good working partnership. She proceeded to speak with a family member who just happened to be a lawyer. He had his own opinions about the contract and told our interviewee, "I think you can get a better percentage, here and here." It became an exercise in comparing apples to apples, based solely on the language in the contract. Where they failed was in not looking at the individual practice to see what it had to offer that set it apart from the others.

Here we have a good dentist who had a lot going for her but she made, we believe, a costly mistake in choosing to commit to a practice that didn't offer her the opportunities that others might have. Whether it was our practice or another, she missed out on working in an environment with all of the tools in place that would have allowed her to flourish, be profitable and ultimately be successful.

It's important for new dentists to know all of the variables at play, so they can make an informed and educated decision, rather than simply looking at the short-term bottom line, which can lead to having to give up a bigger piece of the pie in the long term.

I hope this book educates you on the myriad of options available to you and encourages you to avoid making a costly mistake when it comes to what's next after dental school.

Enjoy the book!

To Your Future Success!

Robert A. Lalor DDS

What's Next After Dental School!

I believe that the average young dentist has chosen dentistry because of the advantages it has to offer, but has graduated with a heavy burden of student loan debt. In order to achieve the goals they've set, it's necessary to proceed by making smart and informed decisions.

If you compare becoming a dentist with becoming a cardiac surgeon, it's easier for a dentist to create more of a family-work balance. You can earn a good living in a fun, challenging, and stimulating work environment. The profession provides numerous opportunities to be generous and charitable, even as you're being productive. It can be a win-win-win situation.

On the other hand, it could be just the opposite. Some dentists make decisions without having a good perception of the reality of their aspirations or the profession itself. *I believe that it's vital to be very clear about options and available opportunities, as well as long-term goals as opposed to only considering short-term concerns like paying next week's bills.*

With an informed approach, all of the details will line up and fall into place. Lacking that informed approach can lead to frustration at work, which then affects home and family, finances and a general dissatisfaction with work. This continuously compounds itself. If the individual makes informed, intentional decisions from the beginning, knowing where those decisions will lead, it's much more likely that they'll have a set path to follow to reach their goals. I hope to articulate some of these actions that can help set a path to success for the new dentist.

New dentists **often** begin their careers with preconceived ideas, working from the perspective that "I'm a new dentist! I'm great. I want to take on the world!" They may benefit from stepping back and taking a long-term approach, saying, "**Okay, where do I need to be? Where can I become the best dentist possible in a year, two years, five years, ten years?**"

Tip: Take a Step Back

I would advise them to look closely at each prospective employer or partner and ask whether it will provide the framework necessary to get where they want to be. Will the practice serve simply as a stepping stone? Is it the right place to be? It's a choice that should be made from the correct perspective, one that allows for an educated decision. Approaching it solely from a short-term viewpoint may lead to the wrong decision. I believe that it's important to look at all the opportunities and determine which are genuine.

Why It's Easy to Make a Misstep for the New Dentist

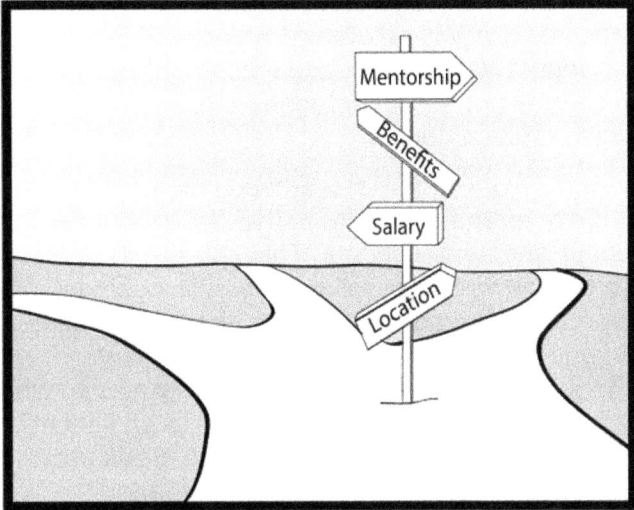

The main problem for a new dentist is that they're just out of school and their loans are due. Therefore, they're heavily in debt, and they're figuratively under the gun to make a decision and sign that contract as quickly as possible. This is made worse by the fact that they don't have many resources to help them or give them good advice. They often turn to friends or relatives who are lawyers for advice, and they don't really have much contact with dentists from a business standpoint. **They may get advice from residency directors who may or may not have business experience in running an office.**

Academics may not be the best resource for practical, real-world advice. Most new dentists lack effective mentors who have the ability to encourage them in the right way.

It helps to find a mentor who is objective, someone with no stake in the game. Looking to prospective employers for advice doesn't work; that dentist has his own agenda, which may not be advantageous to a dentist fresh out of dental school.

There's also a very real-world adjustment for them to make, after eight years in the insulated world of college and dental school. This can sometimes lead to a narrow view, as well as a lack of looking around to see what's available. They've completed four years of college and four years of dental school. For example, we once had a graduate who was unwilling to drive even an hour to an interview. There's a mentality of not wanting to break out of their habits to explore options and broaden horizons, because it's stressful and overwhelming. When they do that, they could miss great opportunities.

Sometimes they have a closed, negative mindset, and many fear the unknown. They've probably heard numerous horror stories in which an evil practice takes advantage of a new graduate. That's added to the mix that leaves them feeling that they have no reliable sources for advice. Add to that a limited skill set, a lack of experience, and uncertainty about where to gain either one, and you could have a disaster waiting to happen.

The 4 Ideal Outcomes for the New Dentist

First, the new dentist would land on their feet at a location that would give them the opportunity to relieve some financial stress, and have the ability to pay down student loans quickly and efficiently.

Secondly, we believe having a trusted and capable source of **mentorship** is vital. Students really don't have to cope with making life-changing decisions; the bulk of their decisions and planning is done for them, and they're monitored all throughout their schooling. It takes a good mentor to help make the transition from school to the "real world", someone who can provide answers to all of the inevitable questions. The difference is that a mentor is not providing constant grading, guidance, and monitoring.

Third, those interested in pursuing specialties – root canals, fillings, crowns, restorative, and so on – should seek out practices that emphasize those specialties. They should select practices that fit their needs, ambitions, and interests. These are the best places to develop a skill set.

Finally, they should be in a place where they can feel proud of the group and the practice with which they're associated. They should avoid any group, individual or practice that may be a source of embarrassment or a damaged reputation.

Covering all of these criteria, as well as whether the work/personal life balance is optimal, will result in a good mix that allows for de-stressing and growth, which adds up to an ideal situation.

Mentorship is vital for the majority of graduating students. In a group practice, there are people who will lend them a hand so they're not working alone. In our environment, we continuously bounce ideas off each other. You're still bouncing ideas 10 years, 20 years, and even 40 years later. You're constantly trading ideas with those around you to gain perspective and better understanding. We hope to get a better result by doing that.

For example, we might have an interdisciplinary case. Recently a patient was about to lose some teeth, so they have surgical, possibly orthodontic, restorative - like fillings and decay - and cosmetic needs. It's necessary to link all of these disciplines. This line of thinking is covered in dental school, but we have certain people who are good at one discipline, and others who cover the others. You confer, and come up with a plan that encompasses all of the experience of the multiple providers in the plan, rather than one driven just by a single individual's personal experience, which can limit you and short-change the patient.

The other day, we had a patient with a "weird" toothache. We could not figure it out. The patient was in tears, and we felt terrible, but it appeared that nothing was wrong. Three of us conferred to reach a diagnosis **which was ultimately the best thing for the patient as well as the doctor who was unsure. Imagine getting stuck on an extraction on a Friday night, it's nice to have a second set of hands to help you out (or call the oral surgeon!)**

As practitioners, we all get stressed out. People who join our practice after being on their own for a long time think it's invaluable to have a colleague to run things by.

Early in my career, I learned some important patient management procedures from my father. You might have technical knowledge, but actually communicating with and helping the patient understand what you're telling them is an entirely separate skill. Providing the patient with an understanding of the treatment, demonstrating that it's the most appropriate course of action, and directing their choices is a skill that comes from experience, rather than from sitting in a classroom.

The 8 Must-Haves Every Dentist Should Know

Must-Have Number One: Three Types of Opportunities.

In corporate dentistry, you're placed in a satellite location which attracts patients by advertising. You're expected to treat them. There is little to no mentorship.

Small practices with one or two doctors and established patients, hire new dentists to take over when the original doctors leave the area or retire. The new dentist receives some training, and the original doctor or doctors then hand over the reins to the practice. It's then up to that new doctor to carry on the practice, which can be highly challenging and even risky.

Larger group practices offer new dentists an existing structure. There's a system in place; patients are accustomed to seeing multiple doctors. The newly hired dentist is immediately busy seeing patients. Other doctors are available to offer support and mentorship.

All dental practices are not created equal, which complicates the process of finding the right one.

One will offer something that the other one doesn't and the third one will offer something else again. You can't re-make this initial decision.

I've also noticed that often, once a dentist has made that initial decision, many dentists have the perspective that this is their final decision. They join a practice, and they start there, and the hiring doctor has consistently done roughly $1,000,000 in dentistry. The mindset is that the most a dentist can do is $1,000,000. **That may be the bar that is set and no one will ever push you beyond that.** A group or corporate practice will have an entirely different perspective. Missing a greater opportunity **because you are stuck with a small mindset** is a common occurrence.

Tip: Do not think all decisions are final

Let me share with you some of the pros and cons of each type of practice. With a small practice, there may be one or two dentists who typically are planning to reduce their workload or retire. The new dentist looks forward to some mentorship, and there may be some, but the doctors typically begin to cut back on the time they're in the office. The mentoring aspect is then lost, and that new dentist is now on her own, perhaps before she's fully ready.

In the corporate dentistry model, the goal is to maximize the facility, which often leads to minimizing staffing. A single doctor could be expected to cover perhaps 70 hours a week. Mentorship is low; staff support, such as billing and insurance, is high. However, dentists are often stuck making their own decisions, and the model usually calls for an emphasis on profits. The dentist can be left in a questionable ethical position. That is certainly not the case in every corporate practice, but it is in some, and it's hard to know which to choose.

In a group practice, there are numerous doctors, so there is a potential for good mentorship relationships and collaboration with partners. Also, multiple doctors bring multiple strengths and specialties. These practices may also offer better tricks and tools, because the practice breaks up costs among multiple providers. The emphasis on the bottom line may not be as strong as in a corporate practice. The multi-group practices place greater emphasis on providing patients with good dental care, using high-quality materials. As you can see all groups are different.

Must-Have Number Two: Using Mentors to Grow.

Having mentors available is invaluable **to me.** Working alone means that an inexperienced dentist is relying on textbook knowledge, which could lead to mistakes. **Even an experienced dentist needs advice.** Having access to that second opinion from a mentor can be of major help, and this is available in a practice with multiple dentists.

Solo practices are just that – solo. You are it, no one to call or ask for advice on a difficult case.

In a corporate practice, the only available mentorship is through continuing education. **One may be also encouraged to follow corporate guidelines rather than discuss comprehensive treatment**

Must-Have Number Three: A Team Devoted to Your Success.

It's important that your team is devoted to your success, that they genuinely want you to succeed. Some practices operate with preconceived ideas among the staff that actually indicate that they want the new person to not do well. In my wife's first practice, the dental assistant refused to work with a female dentist. The assistant had always worked with a man, and she was creating barriers. Certainly, it was not the most ideal environment to come into, right out of school.

Relating this to a **solo**/small practice, the staff is used to the current doctors, and everything runs well. They can be territorial about a young person coming in to rock the boat with new ideas. This can present a challenge to the younger dentist. **It is tough to gain respect and the staff always tends to defer to the existing owner dentist. This**

trickles down to the patients, leaving the new doctor stranded when implementing new ideas.

In corporate dentistry, you may have a team that has lost incentive; they may be uninspired no matter what. It's a job; they punch the clock. They're just biding their time. Of course, there are exceptions, but by and large, I think the corporate models can lead to the idea that the corporation can handle things and staff members are just there to get their paychecks. **The patients may often loose with a team that is not there to care but are there for the perks of the corporation offers.**

In many small practices, the team members have worked together for years. So if a new dentist marches in and tries to change practices that have been in place for all that time, it does not go over well. Sticking with those established practices is important.

Multi-group practitioners often place emphasis on growing the practice; they win by having everyone do better in and for the practice. Basically, in a small or corporate practice, the staff's attitude can make or break a dentist. On the other hand, in a multi-group practice, the staff may have more incentive to ensure that the individual doctor is successful, because their jobs depend on that success.

Ironically, the staff's influence may be even greater than that of the practice's other doctors, so it can be vital to have the staff on your side. Making sure that they're on your side and that you've got a team that's pulling for you is a much better place to be than having one that's fighting against you.

Unfortunately – or maybe fortunately – success in dentistry tends to be based on your team, and on mutual support. The staff's support is vital; if they're fighting you, it's difficult to keep the practice on track.

Must-Have Number Four: Modern, Updated Facilities and Technology.

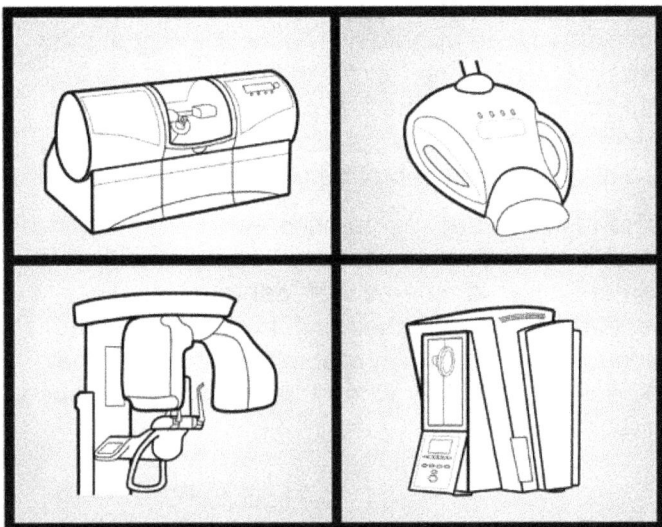

Anyone who graduated from school in 2015 or later wants up-to-date equipment; they're used to working with computers and updated technology. Of course, that can come with a big expense. Corporate dentistry has made the commitment to the expense. Most multi-group practices will also commit to the expense. Small practices might be slower to make that commitment. Some may still work with paper charts, non-digital x-rays, and other outdated technology, just to avoid large expenses.

This can cause conflict between the original decision makers in a practice and the "new guy" who wants to invest money in new technology. An older doctor may want nothing to do with more up-to-date equipment or protocols. They are more concerned with saving as much money for their impending retirement as possible. That becomes a challenge. Compounding that challenge, once the original dentist does retire, the new one is confronted with upgrading the technology at their expense. This is on top of what was spent to buy into the practice in the first place. My advice is to make certain that the practice has been updating facilities and technology before buying in.

When I first joined my practice, which was a group practice, they had no plans to update even something as simple as their dental chair. They were ready to make their exit. I understood it from their point of view. Why would they invest in that expensive new chair when they plan to be finished in four years?

Must-Have Number Five: A Facility Large Enough for Multiple Providers

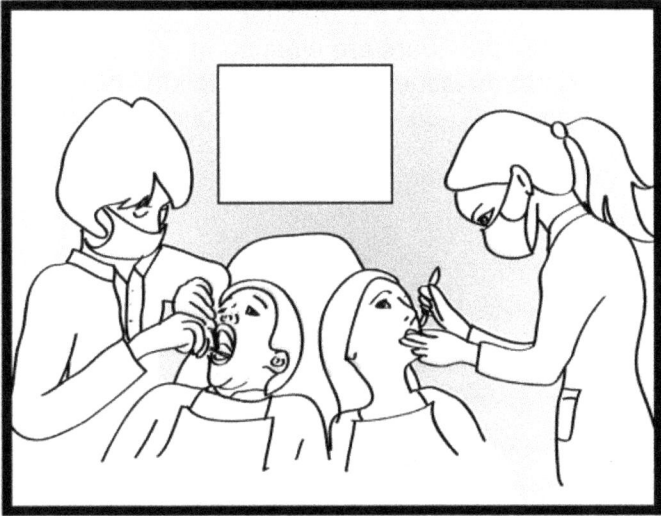

In a small practice, the dentists are very conscious of keeping everything efficient and cost-effective. Chairs and equipment are expensive, so many small practices are equipped to accommodate just a single practitioner. This presents a challenge when a new doctor joins the practice. Many practices divide the day, with one doctor there in the morning, and the other there in the afternoon, which works, but it also effectively eliminates the mentorship aspect. From a practical standpoint, make sure that there is adequate space within both practice and facility.

Corporate-run practices typically try to maximize their facilities as best they can, which often means minimizing the number of doctors with hours that overlap, although practices with extremely busy schedules may have multiple providers working simultaneously. Actual physical space is not a major concern with the corporate model, though.

Multi-group practices are traditionally designed so that multiple providers are working at once, so space is not an issue and it's easy to stay busy and productive.

Must-Have Number Six: Ensuring that Patients Are Okay with Seeing Different Providers.

In a small practice, with a single doctor, patients are accustomed to seeing that one doctor; they may have a personal relationship with him, or they may just be repeat patients, sometimes for many years. If the doctor decides it's time to retire, will the patients stay to see the new one?

Patients of corporate practices usually do not have the expectation that they're going to see the same dentist at every visit. They're used to seeing different providers, so it's not as much of a challenge to gain patients. In corporate, patients might question whether they can trust doctors and staff members alike, because they aren't familiar with them.

Multi-group practices do have patients that are loyal to certain individual doctors, but they are aware of the possibility that they may not see that doctor at every appointment. They're comfortable seeing other dentists because they trust the practice. They see the same face at the front desk, the same assistant, the same hygienist, so they trust the team.

Must-Have Number Seven: Lots of New Patients.

New patients have not established any loyalty to a particular provider. New patient flow will keep a new doctor busy and give the practice the opportunity to grow. In that kind of environment, the new dentist is able to establish a rapport and relationships with the new patients. This applies to all three models, as long as the other Must-Haves are present.

In a solo practice, the new patients want to usually see the existing doctor leaving a few for the new doctor.

Corporate practices usually cater to New patients who do not necessarily care who the provider is which may make for a less that caring relationship as they are usually there for insurance reasons.

In a group practice model that is growing, the patients are there for the reputation of the practice not just one provider. They – if they are a growing and vital practice – should have an ample number of patients who are used to seeing different providers that are reputed to be good.

Must-Have Number Eight: Systems that Guarantee Success.

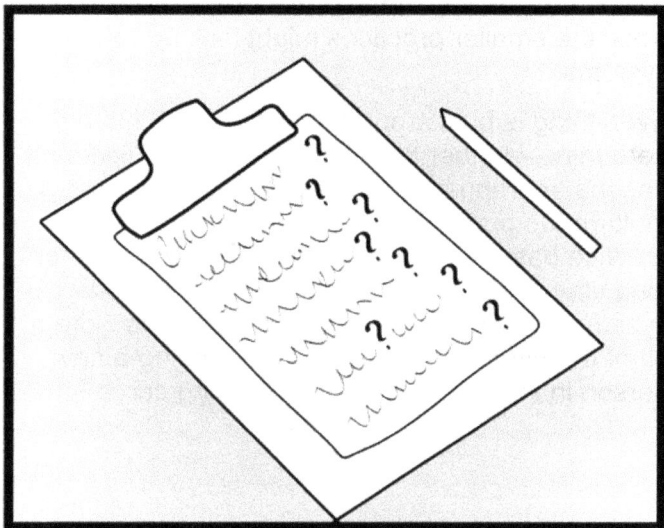

Practices and systems allow you to be successful. In many single doctor practices, the systems are designed just for the individual doctor that is there, but when a second doctor joins the practice, there's a limitation. Will the new doctor do things in the same way? Is any plan in place for adding providers to the practice? This can be a good indication of your expected level of success.

Corporate practices excel here, spending money, time, and effort to determine the best system for making money on each patient. The doctor is often, **however**, just one cog in the wheel.

The multi-group practice will have the benefits of systems that are successfully in place for multiple doctors, along with the benefit of maintaining doctor-patient relationships that are so valuable in the small-doctor practice. They'll have great systems that are also patient-friendly. Corporate offices may be less geared toward the patients, while the smaller practices might lack up-to-date systems.

Everything is built around a system. You have to determine whether the practice you're considering has the appropriate systems. Chances are that a multi-group practice has done the work. If the practice has been in existence and successful for a long time, it's probable that they have a good system in place. Corporate practices have quite a bit of turnover. In a small practice, having a new person in there may require a learning curve.

Bonus #9 MISTAKE

The MOST Costly Mistake New Dentists Make

One mistake a new dentist can make is not taking actual data into account. It's important to ask about money, including how much might be made at the end of the first year. Based on data, the practice should be able to project**. This is more important than any percentage**. As educated as dentists have to be, they sometimes just don't ask the right questions.

Ask math questions that make sense to you!!

1. **What was the most productive year for each provider to date?**

2. **What is the projected daily projection at the third month?**

3. **How many chairs are available for me at peak times?**

4. **How many exams can I do (remember in smaller offices, the patients will not see the newbie)**

5. **What is the number of new patients that is willing to see any doctor?**

6. **What is the case average of those new patients?**

7. **What are your projected capital investments in the next year? Next three years? (Is this a practice that is investing back into itself?)**

I cannot tell you how many dentists do not know how to actually run the data and make evidence based decisions. The only piece of advice they ever get is "get 30%". No one takes that further to say find out what the total is.

Example:

30% of 80,000 vs 5% of 1,000,000

Which would you prefer?

Each of the eight Must-Haves was actually developed as the result of a mistake. For example, I have a friend who is six feet, six inches tall. He joined a practice with the smallest operatory I've ever seen. His new partner refused to spend any money to build a bigger space. One, it never entered his mind to look at the actual facility, and not only did he complain about the facility; he complained about not being busy enough, the lack of hours, the patients, his partners. He complained about Numbers One through Eight, none of which he checked into before joining the practice.

I think many tend to rush making quick decisions based on location, while ignoring important business-related aspects. They seem to think that just being a dentist is going to guarantee their success. But Numbers One through Eight are often stronger determinants of success, rather than location or simply being a dentist. It's important to step back and look at the big picture. Look at all eight Must-Haves rather than concentrating all of your attention on one. If you go down our list, you can find mistakes that have been made for all eight points.

Our experience has been it takes having all of these eight points coming together to be successful. In our practice, we've had doctors who have been very productive and very successful. One of our dentist is far surpassing what he thought was possible in just six months, without having to sell dentistry or jump through hoops. He works hard, sees numerous patients, and makes money. He's far ahead of the game.

Looking back, we have people who after seven years or so have been very successful. They tell us, "I look at my peers, and they're changing from job to job. They can't find what they're looking for." To succeed, you need all eight tips to come together, and it takes more than just showing up to do it. They have to actually work! They have to continue to get better, to work at learning new things. However, at the same time, it's much more rewarding to be in a place where people support you.

How to Ensure Your Success by Joining a Group Dental Practice

This book describes our philosophy in terms of what makes us successful. We have all of the Eight Must-Haves **(and bonus 9th)** in place. We're a multi-doctor group practice. We all work together, in upgraded facilities. We believe in having a treatment philosophy to discuss with new dentists is critical. It's important for the new dentist to have a philosophy in common with that of the overall practice. No matter what type of practice it is, if philosophies are not in agreement, success probably is not a possibility.

The important thing is to develop a philosophy that outlines how we treat our patients, our team, and the other people we work with. Be sure to read our next book, which will explain our practice's philosophy. If that's the right fit for you, and you liked what you see here, we can go into some more intensive discussions on topics like contracts and so on. I think the most important thing is to decide whether you're a good philosophical fit for this type of practice.

If you're interested we would start by giving you a tour of our facilities, and then have you take a few indexes to understand where you're coming from, learn about your personality, strengths, and weaknesses. Then we would have a frank discussion about being where you want to be, about exploring all of the negatives and positives of joining our practice. If we find that you're a good fit, the next step is some mentoring activities and an orientation period. Once past an observation period we set you up to be successful. By the time you actually begin working with patients, you know our system, and you can start putting it into place for yourself. Our staff is there to support you and each staff member has the incentive to make you successful. We should point out that we don't just accept anyone.

If you are interested, you can email us at **projects@lalordental.com**. Our website is **www.LalorDental.com**.

Here's How to Join a Successful Group Practice and Avoid Costly Mistakes

With large student loan payments looming, it's easy to want to jump into practice as soon as you can out of school. You only get one chance to pick the right practice for you. Don't let short term debt force you into making a costly mistake.

That's where we come in. We help new dentists choose the right group practice where they can learn and grow their skills as a respected dentist in the field.

Step 1: We invest time learning about your goals and objectives, and give you a tour of our facility so you can see what sets us apart. We'll show you the pros and cons of working with a group practice so you can make an informed and educated decision.

Step 2: We mentor you and provide ongoing support with state of the art treatment available to patients.

Step 3: We surround you with a staff that is committed to your success.

Most new dentists look at the percentages much too soon when deciding on where they want to work.

Now you can join a successful group practice and start your dental career off on the right foot without making a costly mistake.

If you'd like us to help, just send an email to: **projects@lalordental.com** and we will take it from there.

The 4 Ideal Outcomes	Types of Practices	Must Haves	Questions to Ask
Relief of Financial Stress	Corporate	Mentors	What was the most productive year for each provider to date?
Mentorship	Small	Team Devotion	What is the projected daily projection at the third month?
Specialties	Large	Modern Technology	How many chairs are available for me at peak times?
Proud of practice		Facility for multiple providers	How many exams can I do?
		Patients seeing different providers	What is the # of NP that come in and are willing to see any doctor?
		Continued new patients	What is the case average of those new patients?
		System that guarantees success	What are your projected capitol investments in the next 3 years?